THIS BOOK BELONGS TO:
J. Creasey

••••••••••••••••••••••••••••

Table-Top Science:
Primary

••••••••••••••••••••••••••••

About the Author
Linda Allison is the author of many books
for children, including *The Reasons For Seasons* and
Blood and Guts.

Publisher: Roberta Suid
Editor: Carol Whiteley
Design & Production: Scott McMorrow

Copyright © 1997 by Linda Allison

For a complete catalog, please write to:
Monday Morning Books, P.O. Box 1680, Palo Alto, CA 94302
Visit our Web site: www.mondaymorningbooks.com
e-mail: MMBooks@aol.com

Monday Morning is a registered trademark of
Monday Morning Books, Inc.

Permission is hereby granted to reproduce
student materials in this book for non-commercial
individual or classroom use.

ISBN 1-57612-018-X

Printed in the United States of America
987654321

CONTENTS

●●●●●●●●●●●●●●●●●●●●●●●●●●●●●●●●●●●●●

INTRODUCTION   5

CHANGES

1. **GROWING AND HOW!** measuring and comparing   12

2. **CUTS AND BRUISES** watching the healing process   15

3. **NAIL NICKS** tracking fingernail growth   16

4. **SEED SOAK** changing seeds with water   17

5. **INSIDE SEEDS** studying seed parts   19

6. **SPROUTS** growing seeds to eat   21

7. **HUMMUS** changing garbanzos to a snack   23

8. **SEED HUNT** collecting seeds   24

9. **SEED SURVEY** discovering the seeds you've eaten today   25

10. **ALL WET TESTS** soaking up the scientific method   26

11. **SOAKER SURVEY** sorting absorbers from nonabsorbers   28

12. **COLOR BURSTS** testing colored pens   29

13. **SILLY CELERY** how plants take up water   31

14. **FANTASY FLOWERS** predicting how flowers will absorb color   32

15. **PENNY PILING** experimenting with volume   34

16. **SOLID, LIQUID, GAS** the three states of matter   36

17. **GET CREAMED** shaking a liquid into a solid   38

18. **FRUITY JUICE POPS** changing a solid to a liquid and back   40

19. **GROW A ROCK** turning a liquid into solid crystals   41

20. **LEMON FIZZ** mixing up a carbon dioxide cooler   43

21. **PENNY POLISH** a chemical bath for dirty coins   45

22. **CHEMICAL DETECTIVE** identifying the mystery chemical   47

CONTENTS

●●●●●●●●●●●●●●●●●●●●●●●●●●●●●●●●●●●

LIGHT AND COLOR

1. **BRIGHT LIGHTS** discovering different light sources	50
2. **TRAVELING LIGHT** investigating light beams	52
3. **LIGHT STRIKES** finding out if light always acts the same	54
4. **SHADOW MAKING** learning about shadows	56
5. **SILHOUETTES** identifying people by their shadows	58
6. **SHRINKING SHADOWS** finding how shadows change	60
7. **RAINBOW COLORS** investigating rainbow color order	62
8. **BEND A RAINBOW** making rainbows with prisms	64
9. **WATER-GLASS RAINBOWS** comparing rainbows	66
10. **MIXING COLORS** learning about color combinations	68
11. **DOTTY TOP** finding out if "seeing is believing"	70
12. **DOTS CRAZY** studying the dots of color in photographs	71

WIND AND WEATHER

1. **WIND THINGS** making a wind watcher's sculpture	74
2. **RUNNING KITE** making a kite for windless days	75
3. **BALLOON JETS** creating wind-powered racers	76
4. **WIND SPEED** using the Beaufort Scale	78
5. **WINDY PINWHEELS** wind-spinning fun	81
6. **WIND VANE** testing wind direction	82
7. **WINDY SURVEY** exploring wind makers	84
8. **TINY WINDS** making a micro wind tester	85
9. **BLOWING HOT AND COLD** learning about hot and cold	86
10. **TEMPERATURE TRACKING** learning about "hot on top"	90
11. **SNAKES** making a heat-powered paper snake	92
12. **BALLOON BAROMETER** testing air pressure	93
13. **WEATHER STATION** being a meteorologist	95

Introduction

Table-Top Science is a hands-on set of explorations where everyone gets a chance to be a scientist. Each of the book's three units is organized around a theme: changes (chemical, water, and seeds), light and color, and wind and weather. Each activity is meant to be a short lesson. Adult help will be necessary for some of the activities that involve cooking or cutting.

Each unit's activities build on each other, but they may be done separately or out of order; the activities in each subtheme of the "Changes" unit are best worked as a group since they loosely relate to each other. Activities can be left out if there isn't time, if they don't seem appropriate, or if their focus isn't of interest (science should never be boring!). No doubt you will have your own ideas, too; feel free to add activities to any unit.

The scientific method the explorations follow is presented in an informal way. It is, simply, make a guess, then make a test, then see what happened. Recording sheets to be used in Science Books are provided for some experiments. When questions present themselves, make up experiments and try to get the answers using the scientific method. Remember that science is a process, not a result.

Most of the materials should be easy to find. A list of special materials and equipment that are needed for some of the activities follows, along with covers for Science Books (with space for the scientist's name) and pages to reproduce.

As the children investigate and explore, encourage them to have fun—and remind them that in science there are no failed experiments!

Activities

Each activity will include some or all of the following parts:

IDEAS TO THINK ABOUT

Questions to get the children started; things to consider; prompts to help the children find out what they know, what they don't know, and what they would like to know.

EXPERIMENT

This section asks the children to:
1. Make a hypothesis (the big scientific word for "guess");
2. Test their guess;
3. See what happened.

They might end up with a conclusion but very likely discover some things that lead to more questions.

MORE TO EXPLORE

More questions to pursue if there is time, or time for a child to explore his or her own questions.

WHAT'S HAPPENING

This section offers explanations, background concepts, and vocabulary definitions. Of course very young children don't need to know words like capillary action, meniscus, or phase change, but it's fun for them to use big scientific words.

AMAZING FACTS

Special bits of information that add to the investigation.

EXTENSIONS

Related activities to try in other subject areas, and family activities to do at home.

SCIENCE BOOK PAGES

Use these to track experimental results or make your own books.

Special Materials

"CHANGES" ACTIVITIES:

1. GROWING AND HOW!: students' birth statistics and baby pictures (from home), items of baby clothes and adult clothes, scale, bags, sand, scoop

4. SEED SOAK: film cans, dried garbanzos, warm water

5. INSIDE SEEDS: sprouted seeds, magnifier

6. SPROUTS: seeds, cups, cheesecloth, rubber bands

7. HUMMUS: canned garbanzos, tahini (sesame paste), lemon juice, salt, crackers, plastic knife, blender, bowl, spoon

10. ALL WET TESTS: egg carton; eyedropper; small miscellaneous items, some of which will absorb water

12. COLOR BURSTS: water soluble markers (many colors), paper towels or round coffee filters, cups, paintbrush, water

13. SILLY CELERY: celery, glass, food coloring, knife

14. FANTASY FLOWERS: white flowers like carnations or daises, food coloring, cups

15. PENNY PILING: plastic 35-mm film container or small cup, tray, pennies

16. SOLID, LIQUID, GAS: plastic 35-mm film containers with lids, different liquids, gas-filled items such as soda pop (in a clear bottle is best), a balloon, an air-filled ball

17. GET CREAMED: containers with water-tight lids, whipping cream, marbles

18. FRUITY JUICE POPS: frozen juice concentrate, small paper cups, Popsicle sticks, cardboard, spoon, freezer, measuring cup

19. GROW A ROCK: sugar, Pyrex bowl, boiling water, stick, string, cups

20. LEMON FIZZ: lemonade, glass, measuring spoons, spoon, baking soda

21. PENNY POLISH: dirty pennies, distilled vinegar, salt, cups, measuring spoons

22. CHEMICAL DETECTIVE: dirty pennies, distilled vinegar, salt, cups

●●●●●●●●●●●●●●●●●●●●●●●●●●●●●●●●●●●●●

"LIGHT AND COLOR" ACTIVITIES:

1. BRIGHT LIGHTS: blindfold
2. TRAVELING LIGHT: hand mirrors, measuring tape
3. LIGHT STRIKES: a variety of material samples, such as cardboard, silk, plastic wrap, waxed paper, flashlight or hand mirrors
4. SHADOW MAKING: small items with which to make shadows, light source
or a sunny day
5. SILHOUETTES: black construction paper, white chalk
6. SHRINKING SHADOWS: large nail, cardboard
7. RAINBOW COLORS: pictures of rainbows
8. BEND A RAINBOW: prism
9. WATER-GLASS RAINBOWS: glass, sunlight, metal ice cube tray, hand mirror
10. MIXING COLORS: clear plastic glass, food coloring, pitcher, bucket, spoon
11. DOTTY TOP: stick-on dots, plastic lids, round wooden toothpicks
12. DOTS CRAZY: magnifier, old magazines

"WIND AND WEATHER" ACTIVITIES:

1. WIND THINGS: plastic trash bags, index cards or plastic lids
2. RUNNING KITE: butcher paper or newsprint, string, lightweight cardboard
3. BALLOON JETS: long and short balloons, clamp, straws, string
5. WINDY PINWHEELS: pushpins
6. WIND VANE: corrugated and lightweight cardboard, 35-mm film canister, plastic straw, pushpin, mat knife, clay, compass
8. TINY WINDS: thread, tissue paper
9. BLOWING HOT AND COLD: 3 balloons, 3 identical clear bottles with narrow necks, ice cubes, hot and cold water, 2 Pyrex bowls, 2 jars, food coloring, cardboard, large bowl
10. TEMPERATURE TRACKING: liquid crystal thermometer
11. SNAKES: thread, desk lamp or heat source
12. BALLOON BAROMETER: wide-mouth jar, large balloon, straw, cardboard, pushpins
13. WEATHER STATION: weather page of newspapers, rain gauge, materials made in previous activities

CHANGES

1. GROWING AND HOW!

It is hard to believe how much we change. These measuring activities will let you see and compare how you looked when you were a baby and how you look now.

SMALL AND TALL

Materials
Your length at birth (ask a parent or guardian), measuring tape or stick, string, scissors, tape

1. Measure your height by lying on the floor with your feet against the baseboard. Ask a partner to mark your height with a piece of tape. Cut a piece of string to show your height.
2. Cut a length of string that corresponds to your birth length.
3. Compare the two lengths.

INCREDIBLE HULK

Materials
Baby and toddler sweaters or shoes, adult sweater or shoes, your own sweater or shoes

1. Lay your own sweater flat on a table.
2. Put a toddler's sweater on top of it. How old a kid do you think this would fit?
3. Lay a baby's sweater on top. How old would you be if you could fit into this sweater?
4. Slide an adult sweater under the pile. What differences do you see?

CHANGING FACES

Materials
Baby pictures of you from different ages (the originals can be photocopied and returned home), current picture of you, paper, paste

1. Compare your baby pictures to your current snapshot.
2. Assemble all the pictures on big sheets of paper in sequence.
3. Think about the changes. Has your eye or hair color changed? How do you look right now? Do you think you will change much by the end of the year?

HEFTY BAGS

Materials
Your birth weight (ask a parent or guardian), bathroom scale, bags, sand, scoop

1. Scoop sand into the bags to equal your birth weight. Weigh the bags on the scale.
2. Compare the weight to your current weight.
3. Try lifting your birth weight. Do you think you could lift the weight you are now?

NEW YOU

Materials
Measuring stick or tape, scale, scissors, string, zip-lock bag, sand, paper, crayons, baby pictures and current picture

1. At the end of a year, measure your height and weight.
2. Cut a length of string to show your growth during the year.
3. Fill a zip-lock bag with sand to show how much weight you have gained.
4. Draw things that you can do now that you couldn't do at the beginning of the year. Put the drawings in a book with the pictures of you from the "Changing Faces" activity above.

More to Explore
Make a yarn graph of your height and weight changes. How much did you grow? How much weight did you gain?

2. CUTS AND BRUISES

Human skin really takes a beating. Luckily it is always repairing itself. Watch what happens during the healing process. (Do this activity when you have a cut or scrape.)

Materials
Paper, crayons

Ideas to Think About
How did you get your cut? What did it feel like? What was done for it?

Experiment
1. Make a drawing of how your cut looks right now. Date your drawing "Day 1."
2. Record the changes in how your cut looks every other day. Study the wound and describe the changes. Make new drawings and date them ("Day 3," "Day 5," etc.).
3. What do you think will happen? How long do you think the cut will take to go away?

15

3. NAIL NICKS

Your body is constantly changing right before your eyes. You grow hair, new skin, and fingernails. You can track your fingernail growth if you are patient.

Materials
Paper, colored pencils, measuring tape or ruler

Ideas to Think About
1. What do you notice about your fingernails right now?
2. How do they change?
3. What are fingernails for anyway?
4. Do you have any white spots or dents in your nails?

Experiment
1. Trace your hand.
2. Draw in the fingernails.
3. Measure your fingernails.
4. Mark the lengths on the drawing. Write the date.
5. In about two weeks, measure the lengths again. Mark the lengths with a different-color pencil. Write the date.

Have the lengths changed? Has the look of the nails changed?
In a few weeks, mark their lengths again.

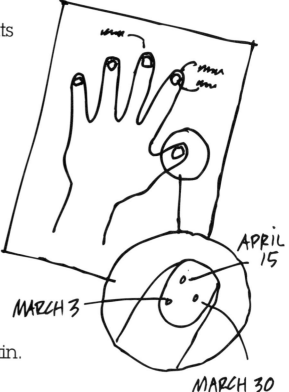

What's Happening
Fingernails act like hard hats for the tips of your tender fingers. And they grow like your fingers are growing. Watch them over a period of weeks and you will discover the rate of their growth.

4. SEED SOAK

Add water to a hard, dried bean and you quickly have a swollen-up seed that's ready to get growing. Try it yourself and watch the change happen overnight, sometimes sooner.

Materials
package of dried garbanzo beans
film cans with lids
warm water

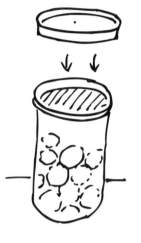

Experiment
1. Fill your film can three quarters full of beans.
2. Fill the can to the brim with warm water.
3. Lay the lid on the top of the can. Don't snap it on; let it rest upside-down.
4. Go away for a couple of hours or until tomorrow.
5. Check back and draw what happened.

Ideas to Think About
What do you think will happen to the water?
What do you think will happen to the lid?
Will all the seeds fit in the can tomorrow

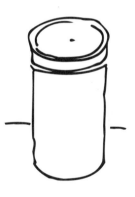

More to Explore
1. Compare a soaked garbanzo bean and a dried bean. What is the difference? What happened to make it change?

2. Fill the film can with soil. Plant one of your beans in the dirt. Add some water and put it in a warm place. Check back every few days for changes.

What will happen to the beans when you leave them out in the air? Predictions?

3. Use the rest of the garbanzos in the "Sprouts" activity. Or cook them and use them in the "Hummus" activity.

17

Science Book Page

5. INSIDE SEEDS

Seeds are space capsules for baby plants. Look inside a seed. Can you find the baby plant? Before you can look inside, you have to soften up the seed.

Materials
Paper towels, clear cup, water, large seeds (a package of soup-mix beans will give you a good assortment), knife, magnifier

Experiment
1. Soak some large seeds in water for a day or two.
2. When the seeds are soft, ask an adult to help you split the seeds in half lengthwise with a knife. Lay the seed halves on some paper towels.
3. Find the baby plant in each seed. Then find the food supply and the outside coat.

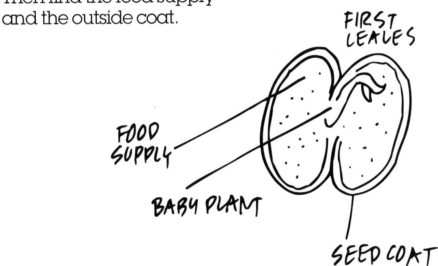

What's Happening
A seed could be called a baby plant that is in a box with its lunch. Packed along with every tiny plant is a food supply of starch and sugar. This food feeds the young plant until it can grow some food-making leaves of its own.

More to Explore
Color the parts of a seed. Cut out the growing seeds. Put them in order. Paste them into your Science Book.

19

Science Book Page

BEAN SPROUT

1. COLOR 2. CUT OUT 3. PUT IN ORDER.

BEAN SPROUT EXPERIMENT

Paste the beans on the page in order:

6. SPROUTS

It is easy to be a sprout farmer. Seeds want to grow—just give them a little water and a few days. Observe these seeds' changes, then harvest the crop for a sprout snack.

Materials
Seeds (try alfalfa, mung, lentil, pea, fenugreek, rye, wheat, lima, garbanzo, or pinto bean seeds), cup, spoon, cheesecloth, rubber band, water, pen

Experiment
1. Put a big spoonful of seeds in the cup.
2. Fill the cup half full of warm water.
3. Cover the top with cheesecloth. Hold the cloth in place with a rubber band.
4. Mark the sprout cup with your name. Let it stand overnight.
5. The next day, pour off the water, leaving the cloth on.
6. Rinse the seeds under running water twice a day. Let the water drain out each time. (If the seeds stand in water they will rot.)
7. Harvest the sprouts when they taste best to you. Some seeds, such as alfalfa, should be ready in two to four days.
8. Have a sprout feast. Try some on crackers that have been spread with cream cheese or eat them on a simple salad.

More to Explore
1. Does sprouting happen faster in a warm place?
2. Can you sprout seeds in a refrigerator?

Amazing Facts
A one-pound (.5 kilogram) package of seeds will grow six to eight pounds (3 to 4 kilograms) of sprouts! Sprouting plants produce a lot of vitamin C.

Science Book Page

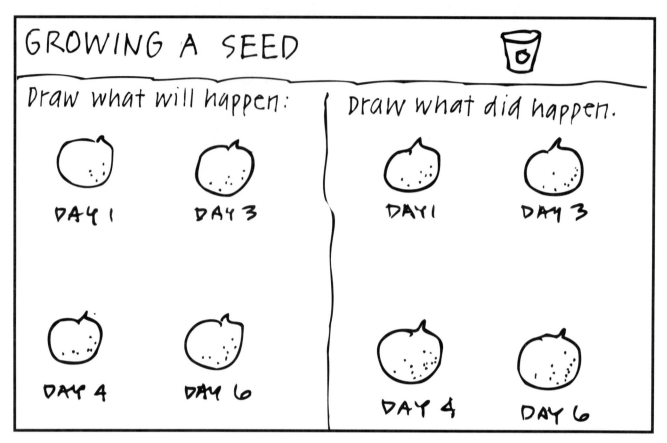
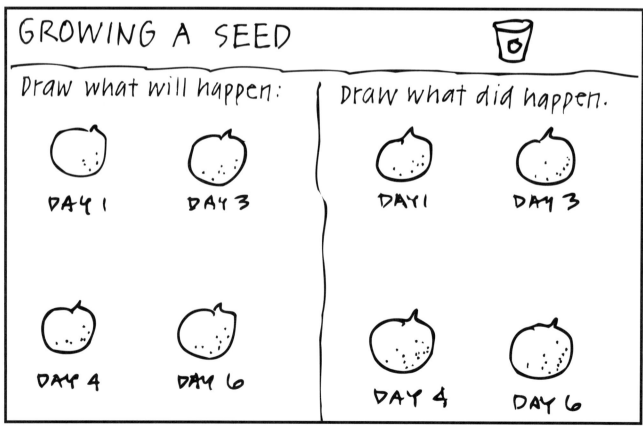

7. HUMMUS

The food stored inside seeds is enough for many days of healthy meals for a baby plant. Animals all over the world have long known the trick of stealing those seedy meals to make a meal of their own. Hummus is a very nutritious spread made from garbanzo seeds and is delicious on bread.

Materials
1 can garbanzo beans, 3 tablespoons (50 milliliters) tahini (sesame seed paste), juice of 1/2 lemon, salt, garlic (optional), blender, bowl, spoon, plastic knife, crackers or pita bread

Recipe
1. Drain the garbanzos. Save the liquid.
2. Blend the beans and all the other ingredients into a creamy spread. Add the garbanzo liquid as needed if the paste is too dry.
3. Spread on crackers or pita bread.

More to Explore
Find a recipe and make nut butter.

Amazing Facts
Both sesame and garbanzo seeds contain a lot of protein. Eaten together they provide more digestible protein than they would if eaten separately. Hummus is an important dish from the Middle East.

8. SEED HUNT

Baby plants are lurking all around your home in their seed suits, just waiting for the chance to get growing. You can find them inside your home and out.* All you have to do is look around.

Survey
How many kinds of seeds can you find at home?
Look in:
>the kitchen cupboards
>the fridge
>a jar of lumpy mustard
>the garden
>the middle of flowers on the table
>your socks after a walk in a weedy field

How many can you find? Ask an adult to help you find some.

More to Explore
Make a seed collection. Do you know the names of the plants the seeds came from?

*Fall is the best time to collect seeds outside.

9. SEED SURVEY

How many seeds have you eaten today? None? Think again. Seeds are a big part of most people's diet. You may not realize that you are eating a lot of seeds because cooking changes their shape. Survey the food you eat. You will find seeds are not just for the birds.

Ideas to Think About
Bet you ate seeds today. Bet you ate them more than once. Rice Krispies? Corn Flakes? Cheerios? Oatmeal? All made from seeds. Toast or muffins? They're made with flour ground from wheat seeds. Pasta? Ditto. Jelly donut? Wheat flour and berry jam are both made from seeds. Coffee cake with coconut? Coconuts are seeds. In fact, all nuts are seeds. Hot chocolate? Made from beans and beans are seeds. Eggs? Not unless you cooked them in margarine. Margarine is made from oil pressed from—you guessed it—seeds.

Survey
How many foods can you find at your home that are made from seeds?
1. Make a list. Draw what's on it. Bring in samples.
2. Sort the seed samples. Make a chart with a column for each kind of seed, such as wheat, oats, soy.

10. ALL WET TESTS

Seeds soak up water. Another way to say this is that seeds absorb water. But seeds are not the only things that will absorb water. Do a real science experiment to find out more about absorbing changes.

Ideas to Think About

"Hypothesis" is a big word that scientists use a lot. All it really means is "guess." Scientists make guesses about what they think will happen. Then they test their guesses with experiments to find out if they were right. All Wet Tests are good ways to learn about scientific experiments.

Before you begin the experiment, think about these things: What happens when you spill milk on a table? What happens when you put a paper towel on the spilled milk? The purpose of the experiment is to test which things are good absorbers and which are not. Do you want to make any predictions?

Materials

Egg carton (plastic is best), water, eyedropper, assorted items to test (bits of sponge, foil, cotton, buttons, dice, bottle caps, cloth, plastic, paper clips, etc.)

Experiment

1. Put one thing in at least six of the egg carton sections (you can fill all twelve if you want).
2. Use the eyedropper to drop some water on each thing.
3. Record what happens.

More to Explore

What material absorbed the most water? The least? None? Sort the items into two groups—absorbers and nonabsorbers. Which group would you make a raincoat out of? Which group would you wipe up a spill with?

26

Science Book Page

11. SOAKER SURVEY

There are many things that absorb. But what things can you think of that really absorb? What do you grab to mop up spills? What does Dad use to wipe his hands in the garage? What sops up milk?

Experiment
1. Look around for things that are really thirsty, or bring some in from home.
2. Test how much they absorb. Record the results.
3. Make a display of the thirsty things.

More to Explore
Eat an "absorbing snack." Have milk and graham crackers. Try dipping the crackers into the milk. What changes do you see? Why does the cracker become heavier? What's happening? Can you think of any other thirsty snacks?

12. COLOR BURSTS

Paper towel drawing can be lots of fun. This kind of paper has a real talent for absorbing liquids. When colored ink and water are absorbed through a paper towel, the color can change in surprising ways.

Materials
firm paper towels (gas station variety works best)
or round coffee filters (pressed flat)
water soluble markers
paint brush
water

Experiment
1. Make a drawing on a paper towel with water soluble markers.
Hint: a flower garden with blobs of color on green stems is a good way to start.
2. When the drawing is finished, paint the colored blobs with water.
3. Go away for a few minutes.
4. Check back. What happened?
5. Try a different set of colors or make a different drawing.

● ●

Ideas to Think About
Do all colors change the same?
What color changes the most? the least?

More to Explore
1. Pick the marker color you think will change to the most other colors.
2. Fold a paper towel into quarters.
3. Draw a fat dot of color where the folds cross.
4. Refold.
5. Dip the dot of color into a cup of water.
6. Remove when the water soaks to the edges.
7. Hang the paper towel up to dry.
8. What color bursts into the most other colors?

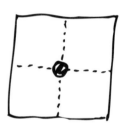

What's Happening
Capillary action that causes water to crawl up tubes causes it to crawl into the tiny spaces in a paper towel. Colored ink from markers is carried along with the water. Different colors of ink travel differently. The surprise is that what looks like one color ink is made of a combination of colors. Chromatography is the name of the science that uses this principle to identify substances.

13. SILLY CELERY

Watch how plants take up water with this silly celery experiment. It proves that water crawls up a thin tube. After you watch normal celery change to silly celery, you can eat the results.

Materials
Celery, glass, water, red food coloring, plastic knife

Experiment
1. Fill a glass half full of water. Add a few drops of red coloring.
2. Slice the root end off a celery stalk. Put it in the water.
3. Come back in about two hours and see how far the red has traveled up the celery. (Cutting into the celery will show this more clearly.)
4. Predict how you think the celery will look tomorrow. Leave the celery overnight.
5. Check your celery. Record what happened.
6. Have your silly celery for a snack.

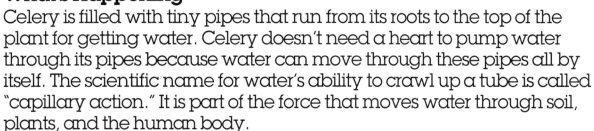

What's Happening
Celery is filled with tiny pipes that run from its roots to the top of the plant for getting water. Celery doesn't need a heart to pump water through its pipes because water can move through these pipes all by itself. The scientific name for water's ability to crawl up a tube is called "capillary action." It is part of the force that moves water through soil, plants, and the human body.

Pour a glass of water. Look closely at the edge. You will notice that water curves up against the side of the glass. The molecules of water are attracted to the molecules in the glass. It is this attracting, lifting action that causes water to crawl up thin tubes.

14. FANTASY FLOWERS

Try some more absorbing science. Make a wild colored flower to wear or give to someone.

Materials
Glass, food coloring, white flowers (carnations or daisies work well), water

Ideas to Think About
What would happen if you gave a white flower a drink of colored water? Think about what you found out in the silly celery experiment. What do you predict?

Experiment
1. Fill a glass full of water.
2. Add some drops of food coloring to make a bright color. Red or blue works well.
3. Cut off the end of the flower stalk (so it's no longer than six inches). Put the flower stalk in the colored water.
4. Check the flower the next day.

Ideas to Think About
What would happen if you gave the flower a drink of pink water? black water? Do your own experiment to find out.

COLORED WATER

Experiment
1. Decide on a color for your flower to drink.
2. Set up the experiment for your flower.
3. Use a Science Book page to predict the color your flower will change to.
4. Color your prediction.
5. Check back in a day to see what happened.
6. Record what actually happened on the Science Book page.

More to Explore
Wrap the stem with florist tape. Wear your fantasy flower or present it to someone.

Science Book Page

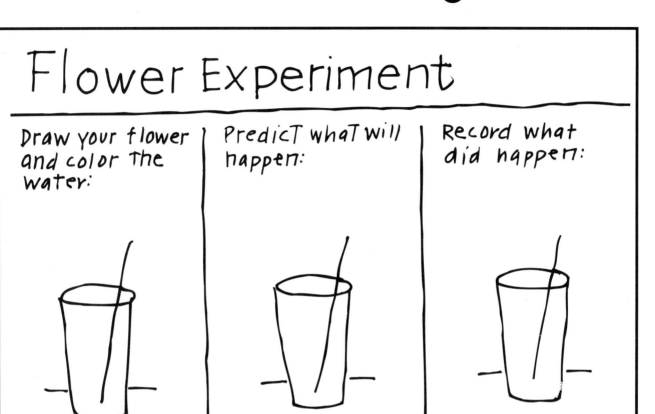

15. PENNY PILING

Drop pennies into a full container of water and watch the water change. Keep count of how many pennies you drop. The number will amaze you. So will water's ability to stack up over the edge.

Ideas to Think About
Pour water into a glass so that it is really full but not overflowing. Do you think the glass is full? Is there room for a penny? More than one penny? How many do you think would fit?

Materials
Film can, pitcher, tray, water, pennies

Experiment
1. Set the film can on the tray.
2. Pour in water so the can looks full.
3. Guess how many pennies it will take to make it full. Record your prediction.
4. Begin dropping pennies into the can. Keep count. Careful not to splash. The can is full when the water first drips down the side. What is changing?
5. Record what has happened.

really full is when it drips over the side

What's Happening
Pennies take up space. The space they take pushes the water up (since there is no place else for it to go). Water is very attractive stuff. It loves sticking to itself almost as much as it likes sticking to the sides of jars. Water's attractive force forms a kind of skin on water called "surface tension." Surface tension allows water to stack itself up over the edge in a rounded shape. The scientific word for this rounded shape that lifts over the edge of a glass is "meniscus."

Science Book Page

Penny Piling Experiment

The film can is full when water spills over.	Guess how many pennies this will take.	Test. Record how many did it take?

Penny Piling Experiment

The film can is full when water spills over.	Guess how many pennies this will take.	Test. Record how many did it take?
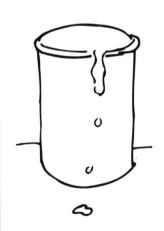		

35

16. SOLID, LIQUID, GAS

Matter exists in three states: solid, liquid, and gas. Matter has the ability to change its state. Scientists called physicists call this kind of change a "phase change."

Physicists are not the only people who care about phase changes. Anyone who has ever waited for water to boil or a juice ice cube to freeze or tried to keep an ice cream cone from melting all over cares about phase changes.

LIQUID DAY

Ideas to Think About
What's a liquid? Where do you find them? What do you do with them? What are they like? Make a list of the properties of a liquid.

Survey
1. Put several different liquids into separate film cans.
2. Pour them into a jar one at a time.
3. Can you guess which liquid each one is? How can you tell?
4. Make a list of properties that liquids have in common.

SOLID DAY

Ideas to Think About
How is a liquid different from a solid? What's a solid anyway?

Survey
1. Set out several different solids.
2. Think about how they are alike and different.
3. Make a list of the properties of a solid.

GAS DAY

Ideas to Think About
What is a gas? How is a gas different from a solid or a liquid?

Materials
Bottle of warm soda pop, balloon, air-filled ball, other handy things that contain gas

Experiment
1. Shake up a bottle of soda and predict what will happen when you take the cap off. Why will this happen? Think of other things that contain gas.
2. Put out a selection of gas-filled items, such as a balloon with air and an air-filled ball.
3. Make a list of the properties of a gas.

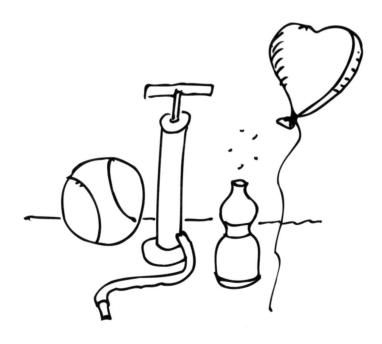

17. GET CREAMED

See, hear, and taste what happens when you shake cream into butter. Changing this liquid to a solid has tasty results.

Ideas to Think About
Have you ever eaten cream? butter? Where do these foods come from? How do you make them? Want to make some now?

Materials
Whipping cream, crackers or toast, clean marbles, small jar with tight lid

Experiment
1. Fill the jar half full of cream. (Chilled cream and a chilled jar work best.)
2. Add two marbles.
3. Put the lid on TIGHT.
4. Shake the jar. Listen and watch what changes.
5. When butter forms, take the lid off.
6. Notice what happened. Pour off the liquid. Spread the solid on crackers or toast.
7. Record the sequence of events.

What's Happening
Cream contains globs of butterfat. Shaking or whipping cream causes the fat globs to grab onto each other. Once the process begins, it starts a chain reaction that separates all the solid fat globs from the liquid in the cream. The separated liquid is called "whey," the remaining solid is pure butterfat.

marbles — cream

Science Book Page

GET CREAMED STEPS

1. Color   2. Cut out   3. Put in order

GET CREAMED EXPERIMENT

Paste the steps in order on this page:

18. FRUITY JUICE POPS

Change a solid into a liquid. Then freeze it back into a solid.

Materials
Fruit juice concentrate like orange or grape, measuring cup, small container, small paper cups, Popsicle sticks, spoon, water, cardboard, scissors, markers, paper, freezer

Ideas to Think About
You are going to make frozen juice pops. Put the juice concentrate into a container. Is it a liquid or a solid? What will you have to do to make the juice pour? How could you make it solid again?

Experiment
1. Decorate the cups with fancy designs.
2. Fill the cups about two-thirds full of water.
3. Spoon in one-third cup frozen juice to each cup.
4. Stir until the juice becomes liquid.
5. Cut several cardboard circles. Put one on top of each cup.
6. Cut a slit in the center of each circle. Put a stick through each circle so it sticks into the juice. Ask an adult to help you.
7. Put the pops in the freezer. What will happen? Draw your prediction.
8. Tomorrow, treat yourself and your friends to your solids for a snack.

19. GROW A ROCK

Make a solid disappear into a liquid by dissolving. Watch water slowly evaporate, leaving behind solid crystals that are a sweet treat to eat.

Materials
Sugar, hot water, heat-proof bowl, spoon, clear cups, sticks, tape, markers, string, scissors

Experiment
1. Fill the bowl two-thirds full with very hot water. Ask an adult to help you.
2. Stir in a big spoonful of sugar. Stir until the sugar has dissolved. Keep count how long it takes just for fun.
3. Keep adding spoonfuls of sugar until no more will dissolve no matter how hard you stir.

Ideas to Think About
Where do you think the sugar has gone? What test could you do to find out if it is still there?

Experiment (continued)
4. Pour the sugar water into the cups.
5. Tie a piece of string around each stick. Wet the strings.
6. Put the end of each string into a cup. Place the cups in a warm place to speed evaporation.
7. Over the next couple of days, watch the water evaporate and crystals form.

To grow good-sized crystals, you have to wait about a week. You may need to break the crust of crystals that form on the surface to keep the water evaporating.

41

What's Happening

Water has the power to take apart, or "dissolve," sugar crystals. (Look at those white grains in a sugar bowl with a magnifier and you will find that they are crystals.) As the water evaporates, it leaves behind the sugar solids. Some solids, such as sugar and salt, have an atomic structure that forms in a magically regular way, making a crystal.

Evaporation is a phase change all by itself. Water disappears into the air, changing from a liquid to a gas.

Extension

One way that scientists record things is to write formulas. Writing a formula is fun. Record the rock candy formula in a notebook.

20. LEMON FIZZ

Change lemonade to a fizzy, foamy drink with a little chemical magic. Use baking soda and the acid in lemon juice to make a gas.

Ideas to Think About
How many solids can you see in the room right now? How many liquids? The third form of matter is gas. Can you see a gas? Not usually. But gases are easy to feel. Blow up your cheeks, then press on them. The air that comes shooting out of your mouth is a gas. So is the stuff you pump into bike tires. Can you think of any other gases? It is easy to see a gas in a liquid because it makes bubbles, like in this lemon fizz experiment.

Materials
Lemonade, baking soda, clear cup, measuring spoon, spoon

Experiment
The baking soda you are going to use is a chemical that most people have around the house. What do they use it for? You are going to use it to make a gas. You will be able to drink this chemical change.

1. Fill half a cup with lemonade.
2. Measure about 1/4 to 1/2 teaspoons (2 to 3 grams) of baking soda.
3. Add the baking soda to the lemonade.
4. Stir the lemonade and watch closely.
5. Taste the lemon fizz before the bubbles vanish.
6. Write a chemical formula to record the results.

What's Happening

Where did the bubbles come from? Where are they going? Baking soda is a chemical compound of carbon, sodium, hydrogen, and oxygen. It reacts with the acid in lemonade to make carbon dioxide gas, which shows up as a flurry of bubbles.

There are many chemicals in the world. Some are safe, some are dangerous. You should be careful handling any chemical. Handle only chemicals you KNOW are safe.

More to Explore

Chemicals act differently with different substances. What do you predict will happen if you stir baking soda into water? vinegar? limeade?

21. PENNY POLISH

Here's a nifty chemical change that will turn old, dirty pennies shiny and bright. Have an adult help you mix up the chemical concoctions. Work with a partner to find out which solution makes pennies shine.

Materials
Small clear cups, distilled vinegar, salt, water, dirty pennies, paper, pen, measuring spoons, spoon

Experiment
1. Put these chemicals in four different cups:
    Cup 1: 2 tablespoons (30 milliliters) of vinegar
    Cup 2: 1 teaspoon (5 grams) of salt
    Cup 3: 1 teaspoon (5 grams) of salt
        and 2 tablespoons (30 milliliters) of water
    Cup 4: 1 teaspoon (5 grams) of salt
        and 2 tablespoons (30 milliliters) of vinegar
2. Label each cup.
3. Drop a penny in each cup.
4. After 15 minutes, record your results.

Ideas to Think About
1. What changed?
2. What was alike and what was different for all the mixtures?
3. Did all the chemicals act the same on the pennies?
4. Do you think the same things would happen with different pennies? Bring some dirty pennies to class for the detective experiment.

What's Happening
Pennies are made of copper. Copper is a shiny, bright metal. Copper reacts with oxygen in the air to form copper oxide. The dark brownish coating on the pennies is the oxide. The acid in vinegar combines with salt to make a chemical solution that efficiently strips the copper oxide off the pennies, leaving them bright.

Science Book Page

22. CHEMICAL DETECTIVE

Can you find the penny shiner? How can you use what you learned in the "Penny Polish" experiment to find the cup with the salt and vinegar?

Materials
Four cups of chemicals like those in the "Penny Polish" experiment, without labels; dirty pennies

Experiment
1. Set out the cups of penny bath without labels.
2. Drop a dirty penny into each cup.
3. Can you identify the salt and vinegar solution?

Ideas to Think About
Scientists figure out what things are made of by how they smell, look, and act. Scientists who are interested in how chemicals act are called chemists. You have just been a chemist.

47

Science Book Page

Penny Polish

Color the successful penny bath

Penny Polish

Color the successful penny bath

LIGHT AND COLOR

1. BRIGHT LIGHTS

There are all sorts of lights around you. These activities will help you take a second look at them.

Survey
Can you find at least 10 things that make light? Look for light sources on the way home from school, in your house, before you go to bed, outside your windows. Record a list of what makes light in your world.

Ideas to Think About
1. What do you know about light? What do you want to know?
2. How many light sources did you find? What are they?
3. Is all light the same—its color, brightness, and sources? Make categories and sort the lights you recorded.
4. What things that are not manmade make light? (Lightning, fireflies, and static electricity are some.)

Bright Light Survey

Draw or write all the things you can think of that make light.

50

●●●●●●●●●●●●●●●●●●●●●●●●●●●●●●●●

WALKING WITHOUT LIGHT

Experiment
Find out what it is like without light by putting on a blindfold. Work with a partner. Your partner will be the eyes for the team. Use a limited area. The one who is the eyes must know that he or she is responsible for making the other person safe while moving around the space. Your friend's job is to lead you around, letting you touch, move, smell, and experience things without seeing. Try to guess what you are touching and where you are. Then swap positions with your partner.

Ideas to Think About
What do you need to see? What if there were no light?

2. TRAVELING LIGHT

Work with a partner on this fast-moving light-beam investigation.

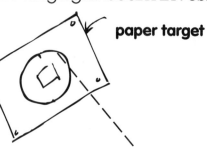

Ideas to Think About
1. Take a mirror and give one to your partner. Investigate your mirrors inside and outside. Can you and your partner discover at least three things about your mirrors?
2. Think about what a light beam is. What did you discover about light beams and mirrors? What do you want to know?

Materials
Mirrors, sunlight, measuring tape, paper targets

Experiment
Play light tag with your mirrors. Work with your partner to shoot light to premarked spots in the room.

Extensions
1. With your partner, try shooting light around a corner using two mirrors.
2. Shoot a light beam in from outside. Your partner has to shoot it to the ceiling.
3. Set up paper targets around the room. Add one or two people to your team and relay light to the target spots. Rule: Everyone's mirror has to be used.
4. How far can you make your beam travel? Predict and measure. Use a tape or measure the distance with paces.
5. Can you reach as far or farther with two mirrors? Predict and measure.

More to Explore

1. Why does the light get weaker as more mirrors are used? Why does light get weaker farther away?
2. Why do you have to keep moving the mirrors to keep the light on target? Why do you think pilots have mirrors in their survival kits? What makes you think light travels in straight lines—or do you think otherwise? What evidence do you have?

What's Happening

Light gets weaker at a distance because light beams spread out as they get farther from the source. This is true for flashlight beams as well as star beams (it's why faraway stars look dimmer).

Light travels from the source outward in straight lines. (Ever notice a flashlight beam in the dark or a searchlight?) When light strikes a surface and bounces off, it is called "reflection." A mirror is a very good reflector because its even, smooth surface bounces a lot of light back in an even, efficient way.

Sun motion seems imperceptible until you try to fix a light beam. You will be impressed at how fast the sun travels across the sky.

3. LIGHT STRIKES

You know what happens when light hits a mirror. But what do you think will happen when light hits a sheet of cellophane? a sheet of waxed paper? a book? Does light always act the same when it hits something? Predict and experiment. Look up the words "clear," "opaque," and "translucent."

Materials
A flashlight or bright sunlight, a collection of things that you think will react differently with light (try waxed paper, glass, plastic wrap, mirrors, shiny things, foil, frosted plastic, silk, cardboard, tissue)

Experiment
1. Work with one or more friends.
2. Pool the things that you collected.
3. Make a prediction sheet.
4. Predict if each item is a light stopper, bouncer, passer, or in between. Record your predictions.
5. Test each item with a beam of light. Record the results.

More to Explore
Can you guess by looking if a material will be opaque, clear, or translucent when light shines on it? How can you tell? How about a balloon—will it be opaque or translucent? How does thickness affect a material's light-passing qualities?

What's Happening

Light behaves differently when it bumps into different materials:

a. Clear or transparent materials allow light to shoot through them.

b. Opaque things block light. Opaque things are solid, although sometimes they have reflective or shiny surfaces.

c. Translucent things let some light through, making a diffused light.

Extension

At home, use a flashlight to see if any parts of your body are clear. Are any translucent, or are you totally opaque?

experiment in a dark room

4. SHADOW MAKING

What do you know about shadows? What makes a shadow happen? Can you shape a shadow?

Materials
Pencil/marker, Shadow Paper, collection of items that relate to Shadow Paper (paper clips, pushpins, crayon, film can, cardboard rectangle), bright light source (outside with overhead sun is best)

Experiment
Can you predict what things made the shadow shapes on the page?
1. Guess and write what you predict made the shadows.
2. Test your predictions. Use the items provided to make shadows to match the shapes on the page.
3. When you make a match, record the results.
Did you always guess right? Can you always identify a thing by its shadow? When is it hard? When is it easy?

What's Happening
When a shower of light hits an opaque object, the light is stopped. The hole in the light is called a shadow. It is interesting to note that shadow outlines of objects are often very different than our idea of what they should be. Hands can look more like birds and bunnies than fingers and wrists.

Extensions
1. Find a shadow of something interesting and trace it. Give it to a partner and see if he or she can guess what it is. Try to fool your partner.
2. At home, try making shadow animals against the wall. Get someone to help trace the funniest one.
3. Figure out how to make different kinds of shadows: a big shadow, a small shadow, a fuzzy shadow, a crisp, clear shadow.

Shadow Paper

5. SILHOUETTES

This investigation is all about people and their shadows, called silhouettes.

Ideas to Think About
How do you recognize a person? Do you think that you could recognize a person by his or her shadow alone? Make a guess. How could you find out if a shadow is enough?

Materials
Scissors, tape or pushpins, head and shoulder silhouettes of several people you know (you will need adult help to create these; one way is to set up an opaque projector, trace the people's profiles onto black construction paper with white chalk, cut them out, and mount them on light paper)

Experiment
Can you guess a person by his or her shadow alone?
1. Hang your silhouettes with each person's name on the back.
2. Guess who each one is. Make a sheet of name strips. Cut them apart. Identify each head by placing a name strip next to it. Work with a partner if you like.
3. Reveal the true name of each silhouette.
Did you guess each person correctly? How did you figure them out? What feature gave each silhouette away?

What's Happening
Generally the eye sees color, texture, dark and light, and a lot of detail when it identifies a face. Given nothing more than a black shape it can still identify a face—most of the time. Quite amazing!

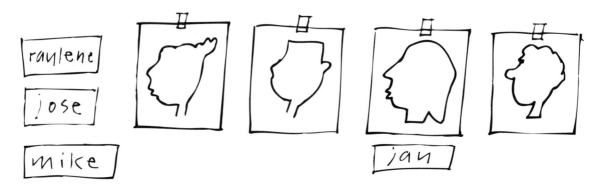

58

●●●●●●●●●●●●●●●●●●●●●●●●●●●●●●●●●●●●●

Amazing Fact

In early America there were no cameras. Silhouettes were the common "snapshots" of the day. Some silhouette artists were so good with scissors they could just look at a face and cut out a likeness—with no drawing needed.

Extensions

1. Shadow Theater: What conditions make the best shadows? Use what you know about shadow making to make a shadow theater. Write a shadow play. Draw and cut out shadow characters. Experiment to make the crispest shadow show.
2. Favorite Thing Shadow: Find a simple magazine picture of a favorite thing, maybe a ballerina, a bear, or a banana split. Staple the picture to black paper. Cut it out. Mount the black silhouette onto white paper.

6. SHRINKING SHADOWS

Does a shadow always look the same? How does it change? How could you find out?

Materials
Big nail, sheet of paper, cardboard (same size), pencil/marker, tape, clock, sunny day

Experiment
Does a nail always have the same size shadow?
1. Tape the paper to the cardboard.
2. Stick the nail into the middle of the paper.
3. Predict if the shadow of the nail will change. If your prediction is yes, do you have any guesses about how?
4. Start early in the day. Take the nail outside and put it in a place that will be sunny all day. Tape down the cardboard so that it won't move.
5. Trace the nail's shadow at different hours of the day. Make sure to record the shadow very early, very late, and at noon.

More to Explore

Ask a partner to help you trace your own shadow the way you did the nail's shadow. Trace it outside early in the day. Remembering the nail experiment, predict how your shadow will look at noon and late in the day. Make at least three tracings and mark the times.

What's Happening

As the sun travels across the sky, the length of a cast shadow changes. What is interesting to note is how much it stretches and shrinks. Early-in-the-day and late-in-the-day shadows are most exaggerated.

Extension

Measure a shadow and graph how it stretches and shrinks during the day. How could you use a shrinking shadow picture to tell time?

7. RAINBOW COLORS

Have you ever seen a real rainbow? Where have you seen rainbows? How could you make one?

Materials
Crayons, paper, books that have photographs of rainbows

Experiment
1. Take a guess about whether or not rainbow colors are always in the same order. Make a drawing of a rainbow from memory.
2. Think about how you could get data on rainbows to check rainbow colors. You could make a series of real rainbows and record the order of colors. How many do you think you would need to make a valid test? Or you could, like scientists, rely on information you don't gather yourself. You might use photos.
3. Take a photo survey. Explore the color order of real rainbows in photos. Record the results.
4. Do your observations show that rainbow colors always fall in the same order or not? How does your answer work with your rainbow drawing?

Science Book Page

Rainbow Survey

Picture 1	Record the colors in order:
Picture 2	
Picture 3	

Rainbow Survey

Picture 1	Record the colors in order:
Picture 2	
Picture 3	

8. BEND A RAINBOW

What's a prism? What can it do? What is it made of?

Materials
Prism, crayons, white paper, tape, sunny day

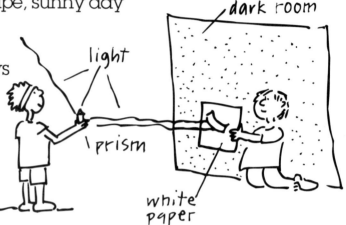

Experiment
Do you think that prisms always make rainbows in the same color order?
1. Make a prediction.
2. Go outside with a partner and experiment making rainbows with a prism. Try catching light at different angles and aiming it at a flat shady wall or floor.
3. Record the rainbows with paper and crayons. Make tracings so that the rainbows are as accurate as possible.
4. Put the drawings up. Which is the biggest? the smallest? How are the rainbows alike and different?
5. Record the results.
Were the colors always in the same order? Was your prediction right?

More to Explore
What if the prism were a different shape? Would you still get the same rainbow colors in the same order?

What's Happening
Prisms bend light. The bending causes light to spread out and separate into bands of colored light that make up white light. Clear substances that have uneven thicknesses, like the edge of a drinking glass, a film of oil on a puddle, or raindrops, can act like prisms. No matter what is doing the bending, the resulting color spectrum comes in the same order.

Extension

Mr. Roy Activity: This crafts project will help you remember the colors of the rainbow. That's because Mr. Roy G. Biv is a handy mnemonic for remembering the colors of the rainbow:

R-red
o-orange
y-yellow

G-green

B-blue
i-indigo
v-violet

It might be fun to collect and think of other mnemonics for remembering important things.

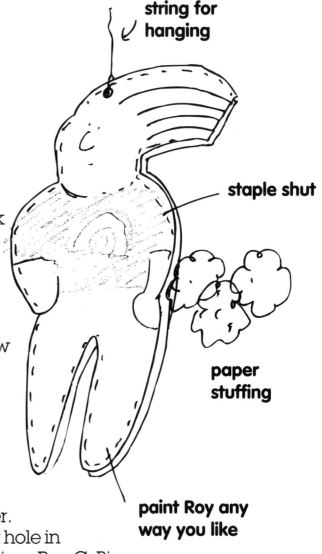

1. Draw Roy on a large sheet of butcher paper that is folded in half. Make sure that the rainbow man has a lot of color and personality.
2. Cut him out (there will be two Mr. Roy shapes).
3. Staple the two shapes together around the edges, leaving a hole for stuffing.
4. Stuff Mr. Roy with wads of paper.
5. Staple the hole closed, punch a hole in the top, and add a string for hanging. Roy G. Biv is a name you'll never forget.

9. WATER-GLASS RAINBOW

With this activity you can make an indoor rainbow!

Ideas to Think About
What happens when light shoots through an empty glass? What happens when it shoots through the edge of a glass of water?

Materials
Different kinds of drinking glasses, water, sunlight

Experiment
1. Set several water glasses on a window sill so that the sun shines through them.
2. Fill the glasses with water.
3. Look for rainbows on the floor. (You will get the best results in the late afternoon with the floor in shadow.) Use white paper to "catch" the rainbows. What is alike and different about how light goes through clear materials? How do the water-glass rainbows compare? List the qualities of different kinds of glass: clear, thick, thin. Make a Venn diagram.

More to Explore
Can you find anything else that bends light? Can you find something that bends light into a rainbow?

What's Happening
Light waves that pass through glass are slowed down. The slowing down creates a bending effect that is called "refraction." Almost any glass jar will bend light to some degree and shoot it off into a different direction. The light patterns created by fancy glasses are no accident. Glass designers go to a lot of trouble to design glasses with different thicknesses and angles to bounce a lot of light. Some glass items have wedge-shaped edges that bend light just like a prism.

Extensions
1. Light Sculpture: Collect glass beads, mirrors, and jars to form into a sculpture. Put the sculpture in a sunny window. Add to it during the year.
2. Wet Prism: See if you can make a wet rainbow.

Materials
Ice cube tray, water, mirror, morning or afternoon light, dark wall

Experiment
1. Put the mirror in the tray and aim it toward the wall.
2. Focus light so that it falls on the wall.
3. Pour in water.
4. Adjust the mirror so that it makes a rainbow on the wall. Why does the rainbow wiggle? Can you make the rainbow bigger or smaller? Any hypotheses about why you see the rainbow? How is this set up like a prism?

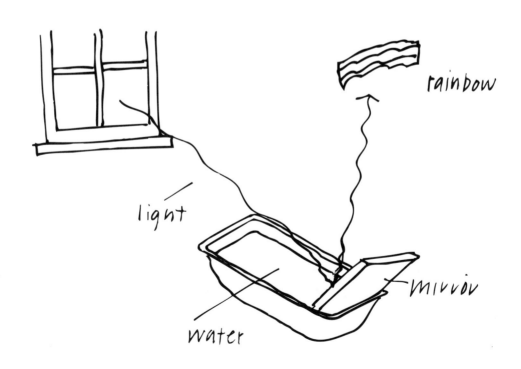

10. MIXING COLORS

Investigate how colors mix together.

Ideas to Think About
What do you know about color? What do you want to know? What is your favorite color? Ever hear of a primary color? What happens when you mix colors? Do you always get a different color when you mix colors? Can you predict what you will get?

Materials
Water pitcher, plastic glass, food coloring
 (the kind that comes in squeeze bottles),
water, spoon, prediction sheet,
buckets for dumping experiments

Experiment
Does mixing two colors always make a new color?
1. Fill the glass half full of clean water.
2. Pick two colors of the food coloring.
3. Guess what will happen when you mix them in the water. Record your guess.
4. Test your guess by adding a drop of each color to the water. Stir.
5. Record what happened.
6. Try testing more two-color combinations.
7. Record your results.

More to Explore

1. What do you think would happen if you mixed all colors together?
2. Mix two colors together. Have a partner mix two different colors. Swap. See if you can make each other's color.
3. Can you invent a formula for turquoise blue?
4. Can you mix all the colors of the rainbow from the three primary colors (red, blue, and yellow)?
5. Work with a partner. Make color mixtures using watercolor on paper. Based on what you have learned about color mixing, can you match a color sample?
6. Mix a color with a drop of white. Add two drops, then three. How many different tints (a color plus white) can you make? (A color plus black is called a "tone.")

What's Happening

Light is waves. The eye sees the different wavelengths of light as different colors. Mixing the red and blue wavelengths causes the eye to see purple.

11. DOTTY TOP

Make a spinning top. Decorate it with sticky dots. Give it a whirl and watch an amazing change. Make all sorts of dotty patterns, then give them a spin and watch them transform.

Materials:
Stick-on dots or stickers (various colors), round wooden toothpicks, lid (heavy plastic with rim works best), paper, scissors

Ideas to Think About
Can you always believe your eyes? Have you ever seen something "weird?" Prove seeing is not always believing.

Experiment:
Make the top:
1. Push a toothpick through the exact center of the lid.
2. Snip off the tips for safety.
3. Give it a test spin. Adjust the toothpick for the best balance.

Test the dots:
1. Add a dot to the top.
2. Record a picture of the top.
3. Do you think you will see a dot when you spin the disk?
4. Spin the top.
5. Record the results.
6. Good work! Try another.

Hint: For more experiments, peel off the dots or cut paper circles and slip these on and off the top. Trace around the outside of the lid to get the correct size.

What's Happening
Spinning doesn't change the dot, but it does change how it looks. When something changes position so quickly, the human eye can't see separate dots. The eye sees only a blur.

Colors change because spinning two dots like red and blue causes the eye to see both colors on the same spot. The eye blends the two together into purple.

70

12. DOTS CRAZY

Have you ever looked at a printed picture up close? Really close? What do you think that you would see?

Ideas to Think About
Investigate color pictures in magazines with a magnifier. What are those tiny dots of color doing in your magazines? What is an optical illusion? What kind of illusion is happening in your color pictures?

Materials
Magnifiers, magazines with color photos, paper, pencil, scissors

Experiment
Can you predict which color dots you will find in a color photo?
1. Cut out a photo.
2. Write your prediction.
3. Test it with the magnifier.
4. Write what colored dots you saw.

More to Explore
1. Can you predict what color dots make a gray area? Can you find an area with no dots?
2. Look at part of a billboard. What do you think it might be? Why are the dots so big?

What's Happening
In the same way that motion can fool the eye into seeing red and blue as purple, tiny blue and red dots blend together in the eye and are perceived as purple.

Amazing Fact

All color photos are printed with only four colors: red, yellow, blue, and black. So only four colors of dots make up every color photo. Can this be true?

Extension

Artists experimented with dots of color at the beginning of this century. They thought the purest color could be formed by dotty paintings that forced the eye to mix its own color. The effects of these paintings are actually quite soft and pastel.

Make some drawings but save a small area in each for a mass of yellow/blue dots to make green or red/blue dots to make purple. Predict whether the dots will work or not beforehand. Stand back and squint when you view your experiments.

Dots Crazy Experiment	
Describe the picture's color:	Predict what color dots you will find with a magnifier.

WIND AND WEATHER

1. WIND THINGS

Build a wind thing. Hang it outside and watch your creation twist and turn in the wind. Wind thing watching will make you notice how often there is wind...and how often not.

Ideas to Think About
Is every day a wind day? Why not? How often do you get a windy day, anyway? Where does the wind come from? Where is it going? What makes wind? What do you know about wind? What do you want to know?

Materials
Index cards or plastic tops (if you want to make waterproof wind things), plastic bags, scissors, tape, hole punch, (optional: mylar ribbon or colored ribbon, string)

Experiment
1. Cut plastic bags lengthwise into strips half an inch wide.
2. Fold a card in half.
3. Tape it closed.
4. Punch holes in the bottom of the card and one in the top.
5. Loop the strips through the holes. Pull them tight.
6. Cut a string about 30 inches (75 cm) long.
7. Loop the string through the top hole.
8. Take the wind thing outside. Hang it where breezes can find it.

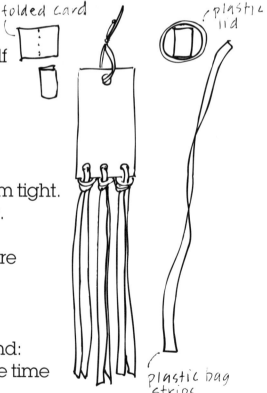

More to Explore
Use your wind thing to keep track of the wind: check it twice a day. Try to do it at the same time in the morning and the afternoon.

2. RUNNING KITE

Argh. No wind again. What to do? Run with this twisty, spinning kite on any windless day.

Ideas to Think About
If there is no wind, can you make some of your own? How many ways can you think of to do this? (What is wind, anyway?) Can you use your whole body to make wind?

Materials
Butcher paper or newsprint, scissors, string, lightweight cardboard, stapler, white glue (optional), markers or paint and brushes, hole punch, measuring stick

Directions
1. Cut two shapes from butcher paper.
2. Staple all around, half an inch from the outside edge. (Or run a stream of white glue around the edge, then stick the two sides together.) Leave the mouth open.
3. Color the kite if you want.
4. Cut a strip of cardboard 20 inches (50 cm) long and 2 inches (5 cm) wide.
5. Staple it to the inside of the mouth to hold it open.
6. Punch a hole in each side of the mouth.
7. Thread a length of string through the holes and use it for a handle.
8. What do you think will happen when you run with the kite? Prediction, please.
9. Take your kite outside to a place with lots of running space. Hold the string and go for a run. Watch what happens. Was your prediction right? What happened when you ran fast? when you ran slow?

What's Happening
Wind is moving air, whether it is a gale or the breeze you feel when you are riding around in a car with the top down.

75

3. BALLOON JETS

Wind sometimes has a lot of force. Use its force to push a balloon racer across the room. Have a race with a friend to see who can make the faster balloon jet.

Ideas to Think About
Blow up a balloon. What's inside that wasn't before? Squeeze the balloon. What is pressing against your hands? What will happen if you let it go? Try it. Can you explain what is happening? Why does it move in a straight line?

Materials
String, long balloons (you might want to experiment with other balloon shapes too), straws, scissors, tape, clamps, measuring stick

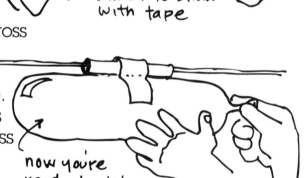

Experiment
1. Make two parallel string tracks across the room. The longer the tracks are the better, but make them at least 20 feet (6 meters). Tying the string to the backs of chairs will work, but stringing them up across the room above eye level is better.
2. Cut a three-inch (7 centimeter) length of straw for each of you.
3. Blow up your balloons.
4. Twist the ends. Hold them shut with a clamp.
5. Tape a piece of straw to each balloon. Some balloons work better with two straws.
6. Put each balloon onto a track by threading one end of a string through the straw.
7. Predict what will happen when you open the clamps.
8. Test the balloon jets by removing the clamps for a second.
9. Give the jets names. Get ready to race.
10. Race the jets against each other to find the winner.
11. Record the results. Show the design, balloon shape, and speed.

More to Explore

1. After the first flight, you might want to take some time to make adjustments. Try: shorter straws, more air, stabilizers, fins, wings.
2. Design the ultimate balloon jet on paper. Draw it, then create it. Describe the parts and why you think it will be fast, based on your experiments.

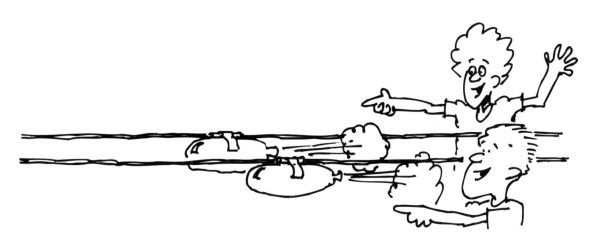

What's Happening

When you blow up a balloon, you are forcing air into a small space. The air inside a balloon is under more pressure than the air outside a balloon. The air inside tries to get even. When it is given an opening, it rushes from the high-pressure zone to equalize itself with the air outside. The force of air moving out the back pushes the jet forward. (Or, remembering Newton's Law: For every action there is an equal and opposite reaction. So air being forced out the back pushes the balloon forward.)

4. WIND SPEED

You can glance out the window and tell how fast the wind is moving if you know how to use the Beaufort Scale. Make a wind chart and learn the truth about the number of windy days in your neighborhood.

Ideas to Think About
Speed is measured in mph (kph). Can you explain what that means? If you were a loose balloon, how far would you get in an hour if the wind was blowing at eight miles (13 km) per hour (assuming you didn't get stuck in a tree)?

Experiment
Some days there is a small breeze, some days a fierce wind. What is different is how fast the wind is blowing.
1. Look out the window.
2. Match what you see to the Beaufort Scale.
3. Record the speed.

Extensions
1. Try some simple time and distance problems. How far would you blow in an hour at Beaufort 3? in two hours?
2. Streamers are a fun way to experiment with wind speed, direction, and force. Cut a long, long strip of crepe paper two inches (5 cm) wide. Take it out in a strong wind and run around. Think about how you could capture the force of the wind to push or pull things.

Amazing Facts
1. In the old days, communication depended on the wind. The great sailing ships carried cargo and mail.
2. Admiral Beaufort invented his wind scale in the 1800s. Wind is still measured in "Beauforts" today.

Science Book Page

WIND SPEED LOG:

Date	What's Happening	Beaufort #	Miles per hour

WIND SPEED LOG:

Date	What's Happening	Beaufort #	Miles per hour

Beaufort Wind Scale

			M.P.H
calm	smoke rises straight up.		0
light	smoke drifts flags limp		1-3
light	feel wind on face leaves rustle flags begin to move		4-7
gentle	twigs move		8-12
moderate	papers and dust blow small branches move		13-18
fresh	small trees move flags ripple		19-24
strong	phone wires whistle flags beat umbrella use difficult		25-31
strong	flags stand straight out whole trees sway		32-38
gale	breaks twigs off trees very difficult to walk		39-46
gale	antennas and signs blow down		47-54
whole gale	trees topple, buildings are damaged		55-63
hurri-cane	widespread devastation		75+

5. WINDY PINWHEELS

Make a wind-powered pinwheel. Capture the pushing power of the wind and turn it into some spinning fun.

Ideas to Think About
People since ancient times have used the wind to power all sorts of inventions. How many inventions can you think of that use wind power?

Materials
Construction paper, pushpins, pencil with eraser or drinking straw, scissors

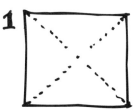
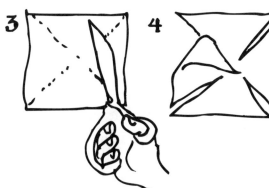

Directions
1. Cut out a construction paper square. A four-inch (10 cm) square makes a small pinwheel. A ten-inch (25 cm) square makes a large one.
2. Fold the square on the diagonal in both directions.
3. Cut along the diagonal lines. Do this about two-thirds of the way to the center.
4. Fold over each corner. Capture each corner with a pin, working around the corners in order.
5. Push the pin into the pencil eraser or straw.
6. Adjust the flaps so the pinwheel spins easily.

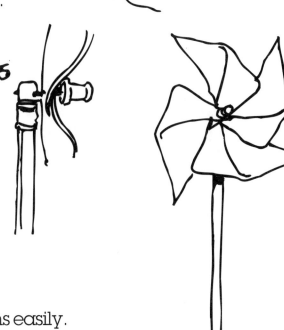

Extension
Put on your thinking cap and make a list of as many windy sports and windy toys as you can think of.

81

6. WIND VANE

You don't need a weather person to know which way the wind blows. All you need is your own easy-to-make wind vane.

Ideas to Think About
How do you tell wind direction? (Look at flags or trees, feel the wind on your body.) Why would you want to know this? What do people use to tell wind direction? Why do people use a wet finger to test the wind?

Materials
Corrugated cardboard, lightweight cardboard, film can with lid, mat knife, pencil with eraser, scissors, drinking straw, pushpin, plasticine clay, compass, paper clips, stapler, glue

Experiment
You are going to make a wind vane that really works. Then you will test it outside.
1. Cut out a triangle and a rectangle from light cardboard (have an adult help you).
2. Slit both ends of the straw (have an adult help you). Make the slits 1/2 inch (1 cm) long. Make sure the slits are aligned with each other.
3. Slide the cardboard triangle into one slit and the rectangle into the other.
4. Staple them in place.

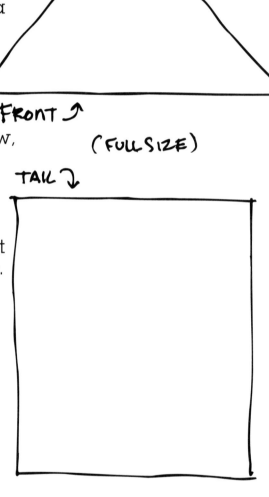

FRONT ↗

(FULL SIZE)

TAIL ↙

82

5. Find the balance point on the straw. Use a finger or pencil. Mark the point.
6. Poke a pin through the straw at the balance point. Make sure the cardboard pieces are on edge straight up and down to the ground.
7. Cut or rub the pencil eraser to a point.
8. Attach the straw to the eraser point with the pin.
9. The straw should turn freely. If it doesn't, enlarge the hole a bit.
10. Cut an X in the middle of the lid of a film can. (Have an adult help you use a mat knife.)
11. Push the pencil point into the slits so the pencil stands upright.
12. Glue the film can to the middle of the corrugated cardboard.
13. Set the wind vane up outside in a level place where wind can hit it from all sides.
14. Mark the corners of the cardboard north, south, east, and west. Find north on the compass. Mark it on the ground with an arrow. Line up the north corner of the wind vane.
15. Read the wind vane. Remember that it points to the direction that the wind is coming from. Record your findings.

Extension

Find pictures of wind vanes. Why do you think they come in so many shapes?

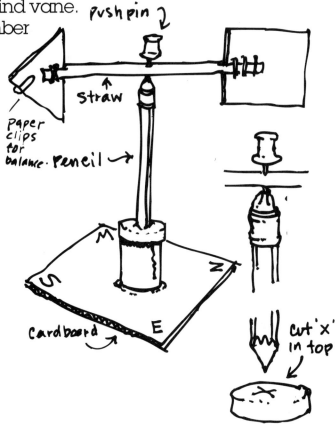

7. WINDY SURVEY

Winds crop up in more places than you might think. Look around. You will be surprised at how many windy things there are in your life—especially if you count manmade wind makers.

Survey

Can you find 10 things that make wind? Look outside the windows, inside the house, on the way home from school. Then record a list of what makes wind in your world. Draw pictures of the things, write about them, or collect magazine pictures that show them.

Ideas to Think About

What did you find in your survey? How many sources of wind are there? Make categories and sort wind makers. Don't forget about machines that have fans to keep heating elements cool, breathing, flipping pages of a book, slamming a door, opening a soda can.

Windy Survey

Can you find six things that make wind?
Draw or write them:

8. TINY WINDS

Shut all the doors. Close the windows tight. You still are not safe from tiny winds that blow around inside your house. Make a micro wind tester and see for yourself.

Ideas to Think About

Do you live in a drafty house? Is your room windy? Do you think there is wind in the room you are in now? Even with the windows shut? Try to find a windless place in the room. Can you find the windiest place?

Materials

Tissue paper, thread, tape, scissors

Experiment

1. Cut a tissue rectangle about one inch by one and a half inches.
2. Cut a thread about 10 inches (25 cm) long.
3. Tape the thread to the tissue.
4. Find a spot to test for wind. Position your tester.
5. Hold it perfectly still.
6. If your tester won't stop swinging, there is wind.
7. Test other spots. Record your results.

Extension

Take your tester home. Can you find the windiest place in your room? Map the windy spots in your room.

What's Happening

Even with all the windows shut tight, you're likely to find wind in a room. Wherever hot and cold air masses come together, you will find the turbulent air currents that we call winds—even on a mini scale.

heat source

85

9. BLOWING HOT & COLD

Here are two experiments to help you discover the driving force behind hot and cold.

BIG HOT AND LITTLE COLD

Ideas to Think About
What makes air move? What makes air move outside? What do you know about the cause of wild winds?

Materials
3 bottles (with narrow necks), 3 balloons, ice, ice water, hot water (almost boiling is best), 2 Pyrex bowls

Experiment
1. Attach a balloon over the neck of each bottle.
2. Set two of the bottles in bowls. Keep one bottle out of a bowl.
3. What's inside the bottles? What will happen if you cool the air in one bottle? What will happen if you heat the air in another bottle? Write down your predictions. Think of ways you might heat and cool the air in the bottles in the bowls. Then continue the experiment.
4. Pack ice around one bottle. Pour in water.
5. Pour in very hot water around the other bottle.
6. What is happening? Why?

What's Happening

When air is heated, it expands. As molecules in air are heated, they speed up and move apart. They take up more space, becoming less dense. Hot air weighs less and so it rises.

The opposite happens when air is cooled. When it is cooled, it contracts. Air molecules take up less space, becoming denser. Cold air weighs more and so it sinks.

HOT ON TOP

Ideas to Think About
What happens if you put two different temperatures of water together? Predictions, please. (Hint: Think about what happened to the two balloons in "Big Hot and Little Cold.") The following experiment will help you find out, first with hot on the top, second with hot on the bottom.

Materials
Hot water, ice water, ice cubes, food coloring, cardboard, 2 jars, large bowl (to catch the overflow)

Experiment
1. Fill one jar with ice water and an ice cube.
2. Fill one jar with hot tap water.
3. Add several drops of food coloring to make a bright color in the hot jar.
4. Cover the hot jar with the cardboard. (Press down to create a suction seal. This will help keep the water from leaking.)
5. Place the cold jar on the bottom in the bowl. Quickly turn the hot jar upside down and put it on top of the cold jar. Align the rims and pull away the cardboard.
6. Watch what happens. Record the results.
7. Carefully flip the jars so that the cold jar is on top.
8. Watch what happens. You will see hot water streaming to the top. You will see ice melting and sending streamers of cold water to the bottom. Look closely, because it all happens in less than a minute. Record the results. You may want to try the experiment again.

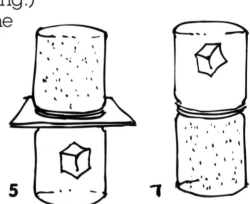

What's Happening

Hot substances rise to the top because they are lighter. Cold substances sink to (or stay put at) the bottom because they are heavier. Turbulence is created when the two temperatures mix.

More to Explore

What do these experiments have to do with wind? When a pilot asks you to fasten your seat belt because of turbulence, what temperature zone do you guess you are in?

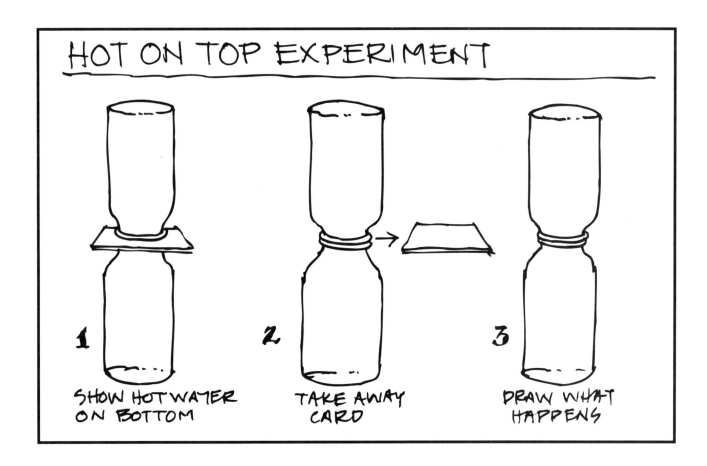

10. TEMPERATURE TRACKING

What's the temperature in the room you are in? Use an easy-to-read liquid crystal thermometer. Discover that your space probably has more than one temperature.

Ideas to Think About

1. What's your favorite weather? How hot do you like it? Do you have a favorite temperature? How hot is too hot?
2. How many degrees do you think it is in the room right now? Take a guess. Record your prediction.

Materials

Liquid crystal thermometer, tape, recording sheet

Experiment

1. Read the room temperature on the thermometer and record it.
2. What if you put the thermometer on the ceiling? Would the temperature be the same? Make a prediction and record it.
3. Tape the thermometer as close to the ceiling as possible (ask an adult to help you). Choose a spot as far away from the heat source as possible.
4. Record the temperature.
5. Predict what the temperature would be if you put the thermometer on the floor. Record your prediction.
6. Tape the thermometer near the floor at baseboard level.
7. Record the temperature.

Extension

Record the temperatures over the next few days.

* Liquid crystal thermometers in a postcard format are inexpensive and unbreakable. They are available from the Exploratorium store in San Francisco. Order by telephone at 415-524-7400.

●●●●●●●●●●●●●●●●●●●●●●●●●●●●●●●●●●●●●●

More to Explore

1. What do you know about temperatures on Earth? What does temperature have to do with wind?

2. Make a map of the room and the area outside showing the range of temperatures that you find. What is the hottest place? the coldest? Where is it between 60 and 65 degrees?

11. SNAKES

Cut out this nifty twisty critter that is powered by micro winds. Put it in the right spot and see in action the theory that heat rises.

Materials
Thread, construction paper, scissors, crayons or colored pencils, warm lamp or candle

Experiment
1. Cut a four-inch (10 cm) circle out of construction paper.
2. Cut a spiral to the center.
3. Punch a hole in the middle of the spiral.
4. Put a thread through the hole. Knot one end to hold it.
5. Decorate the snake.
6. Hang it over the lamp in the closed position.
7. Experiment by gently stretching out the snake to make it longer.

Try it closed... or open

Ideas to Think About
Can you explain what makes the snake move? Where in the room do you think it will spin the fastest? (Hint: Where are you likely to find hot and cold air coming together?) Test your prediction to find out if you guessed right.

What's Happening
It only takes a small air current to jiggle this snake. When you hang it over a heat source the rising stream of hot air sets it in motion.

HEAT SOURCE

12. BALLOON BAROMETER

One of the handiest tools for predicting a change in weather is the barometer. A really accurate barometer is fairly expensive, but you can build your own barometer from simple things that will reflect air pressure and temperature changes.

Materials
Wide-mouth jar (like an empty quart peanut or mayonnaise jar), balloon, heavy-duty rubber band, drinking straw, glue, cardboard, paper, scissors, ruler, recording chart, pushpins

Experiment

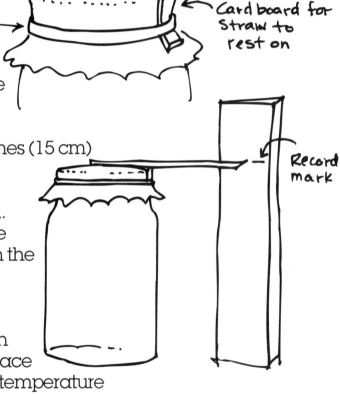

1. Cut the balloon so that it will open flat.
2. Stretch it across the mouth of the jar.
3. Hold the balloon in place with the rubber band. (The jar should now be airtight.)
4. Cut the straw so it is about six inches (15 cm) long. Cut the end into a point.
5. Glue the straw to the balloon, starting at the middle of the balloon.
6. Slip a strip of cardboard under the rubber band. It should be even with the edge so the straw rests on it.
7. Make a recording chart strip to pin to a wall.
8. Set the barometer up on a table in front of the recording strip. Find a place that is out of the sun and where the temperature doesn't change much.
9. Take a reading each day. Mark with a pin where the balloon pointer touches. Each time you record, move the barometer to the next chart square. This is a very basic barometer, so don't expect wild changes in pointer position. The pointer moves just a bit.

What's Happening

A barometer shows changes in air pressure. The air trapped inside the barometer presses up against the balloon at a steady rate. When outside air pressure increases, it pushes down on the balloon so the pointer moves up. When outside air pressure drops, the air inside the jar pushes the balloon up so the pointer moves down.

One look at any barometer won't tell you much. What is important is to check the needle or pointer's position, then come back in a few hours to see if it is rising or falling. Changes in air pressure usually mean a change in weather. Watch your barometer to find out about the weather.

Extension

Compare the movements of your balloon barometer with a more accurate instrument if one is available.

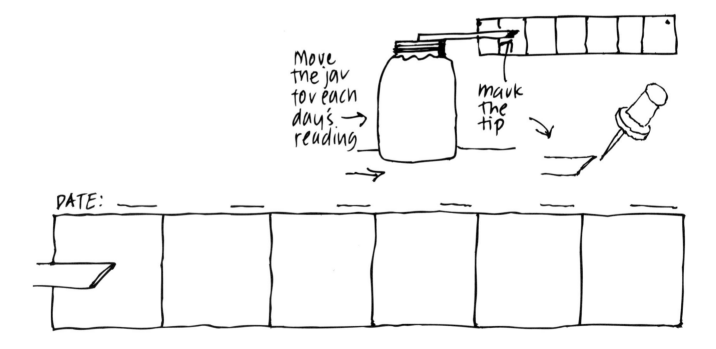

13. WEATHER STATION

If you have tried all the experiments in this unit, you have enough equipment to create your own weather station. Using that equipment, keep a weather log. After a while you might begin to find patterns that will let you predict the weather.

Ideas to Think About

A meteorologist is a person who studies the weather. What do you know about a weather person's job? What do you want to know about the weather and the job? What instruments do you think meteorologists need?

Activity

Make a weather log. Take recordings of the temperature, wind speed, wind direction, air pressure, rain amount, and cloud cover at the same time every day. Try keeping the log for at least a month.

Temperature:
Take your readings out of direct sunlight.

Wind Speed:
Use the Beaufort Scale.

Wind Direction:
Use the wind vane.

Barometer:
Record if the needle is steady, rising, or falling.

Rain:
Look up statistics in the newspaper or use a rain gauge.

Cloud Cover:
Note if the sky is cloudy or clear.

● ●

More to Explore

After a month, you might go back and see if there are any patterns that show up in your weather journal. For instance, is it always windy before it rains? Does the wind blow in any direction before a storm? Is there a pattern to the foggy days? to the sunny days?

Extension

Collect amazing weather stories from the paper. Or read the weather tales included in <u>It's Raining Cats and Dogs: All Kinds of Weather and Why We Have It</u> by Franklyn M. Branley.

WEATHER LOG

Date/Time	Temp.	Wind Speed	Wind Direction	Barometer	Rain